# DAVE MATTHEWS BAND

## by Mark Wood

### JUST THE RIFFS FOR VIOLIN

*Boyd Tinsley*

*Photography by Danny Clinch*

*Also available: Dave Matthews Band Just the Riffs for Sax, by David Pope (02500373), and Dave Matthews Band Just the Riffs for Guitar (02500019)*

ISBN 978-1-57560-460-2

*Visit our website at www.cherrylane.com*

T0056132

# Introduction

When it comes to the violin, tradition calls the shots. There is this one path all violinists follow. We play in the school orchestra, study with the local violin teacher, and then apply to the numerous conservatories. We work on our scales and our etudes hoping to strengthen our technique. And then we apply this technique to learning the "top 40" of the classical repertoire.

Every once in a while, somebody comes along who breaks from this mold and expands the tradition. Boyd Tinsley is this type of musician. He started out on a traditional path, but at some point he hit a fork and took the road less traveled. As an integral part of the Dave Matthews Band, Boyd has brought his violin playing to stadium-size crowds and helped redefine its place in modern rock music. He has consistently developed interesting and innovative techniques; his use of pizzicato and doubling guitar lines and his rock, jazz, and country influences appear in many of band's well-known songs. Whereas Boyd grew up with Jerry Garcia and Neil Young as his influences, you can now look to Tinsley himself as one of your own.

This book is a fun and great way to stretch your vision of the violin. Even though this book is "Just the Riffs," I've also included a couple of Boyd's solos for everyone to experience. So here is your chance to enjoy and explore the violinist's approach to the often quirky and ingenious music of the Dave Matthews Band. Let these riffs inspire you to grow and experiment on your own and follow Boyd down those largely unexplored roads of electric violin playing.

# About the Author

Mark Wood, progressive rock/pop electric violinist and composer, pursued studies at the Juilliard School of Music and at Tanglewood under maestro Leonard Bernstein. Mark has toured and performed with Celine Dion (performing the duet "To Love You More"), Everclear, Billy Joel, Lenny Kravitz, Jewel, the Trans-Siberian Orchestra, and others, and has released several recordings. In his capacity as composer, he has received two Emmy nominations for film and television projects. Mark is the owner and operator of Wood Violins, a company dedicated to manufacturing cutting-edge electric violins—check out his website at www.woodviolins.com.

# Contents

# An Interview with Boyd Tinsley

*Mark Wood: What was your first introduction to music?*

Boyd Tinsley: I was born in '64. I was a kid during the '70s and late '60s. I was listening to lots of the music that was on the radio back then, like the Jackson Five, the Supremes, the O'Jays, James Brown. My older brothers and sisters would bring home a lot of the Motown singles of the time. There was also gospel music because my father was a youth choir director at a Baptist church. There was also an undercurrent of what they now call classic rock—Led Zeppelin, Neil Young, bands of the '70s. I grew up with a combination of all those influences.

*At one point you chose the violin.*

When I was 10 or 11, I wanted to be a rock guitarist. I really stumbled upon the violin when I was going to middle school. I signed up for a class for strings. I thought maybe I could learn to play guitar. I didn't realize until I got to it that it was a string orchestra class. I was like, "What's a violin?" I tried it because I just happened to sign up for this class. There wasn't any forethought at all. It was a complete accident. I guess it was the most fortunate accident of my life.

*What was the turning point for you to say "let me electrify this thing"?*

It was pretty early on. Some of my orchestra conductors turned me on to players like Jean Luc Ponty, Stephane Grappelli, and Papa John Creach. These were some of the older people who were doing non-classical things with the violin—playing jazz and rock. I remember in eighth or ninth grade thinking, "that is something I can do—I can take this and play rock or jazz," which sort of tied into what my passion had always been as a child, which was to be in a rock band. I studied classical music and took lessons throughout high school, and it wasn't until the point that I got to college that I started experimenting with jamming or improvising on Neil Young, Grateful Dead, and Dylan tunes in coffee houses.

*What method did you use to jump from the notation of the classical violinists to the improvisational aspects of rock?*

There was no method at all. It was basically "just do it." It was like growing up speaking English all your life and then suddenly moving to a foreign county and having to learn a different language. When I was in college (University of Virginia), I hooked up with this fraternity (Sigma Nu) and probably 75% of the guys in the fraternity played guitar. They would have these almost weekly coffee house jams, and local musicians would come down and play music all night long. I'd bring my violin, and we would just play and play. I started to realize that I know where the notes are. It's just a matter of testing myself. It was always on-the-job training. I got in there and just sort of did it.

*There wasn't any particular player whose licks you tried to cop?*

No, not at all. To be honest with you, the musicians that influenced me the most were not violin players. Jerry Garcia had a bigger influence on me than Stephane Grappelli. I liked musicians who were more into the jam aspect of playing music. Neil Young was a big influence on me.

*Do you notate on music paper with the Dave Matthews Band or is it all done by ear?*

It's all pretty much done by ear. The one exception is the album *Everyday*. That's the first time there were ever notes involved beforehand and during and at the recording of our music.

*Your use of pizzicato is fantastic. Are there other violin techniques that you find useful from the classical world?*

I do a lot of trills, and tremolos are pretty effective in certain songs in certain moments. I try to take *pizzicato* playing to a whole different level. I had Zeta make a violin for me that I call a Fiddolin. It's made for *pizzicato*. The bridge is a little bit heavier, and its got guitar tuners that stay in tune better. Some tunes that we do I actually strum the violin more like a mandolin or guitar.

*How do you approach writing your violin parts for the songs?*

First of all, the thing to do is to sit back and listen to the song. It's a matter of getting into the song and listening and finding that place. That's pretty much the process that we all take in this band in making all our parts. It basically comes down to listening to the music and knowing where you fit in and where you don't.

*On "Jimi Thing" you do a smokin' solo and outro. How do you approach the soloing to that?*

Yeah. I grew up in a time when rock 'n' roll was in your face, just jamming for what it's worth. I have to go back to Neil Young as a major influence on me because, when he is soloing, lot of times it's just rockin' out and playing that raw feeling that comes out unfiltered. It's very real, and that's the way I come towards music. It's real; it's right now. There is no reason to think about how I can make it more perfect. Some nights, the way I'm feeling is to play something that is a little more melodic or funky or laid back. Some nights it's "grab it by the balls and just go."

*On "The Stone," you use this driving rhythm. You are so smart in exploring that, and when you play it's like a freight train.*

To me, rhythm on violin has been a big thing. A good half of it is being a rhythm instrument. I love getting into that sort of rhythmic riff with Carter, our drummer. Carter is amazing. He can go anywhere on the drums, and it's really cool to get into some sort of rhythm interplay with him. It's always been a part of me, and I like to bring it out in the music on this instrument.

*How do the songs evolve from recording to the stage?*

We want to make it sound as perfect as we can get it in the studio, but live is a whole different thing with us. We started as a live band—as a bar band, basically—playing to live audiences, and you had to rock out. We are not afraid to expand upon our songs, amend them, and change them as they go along because the music to us is always live. We change things up because we grow as a band and we hear the music differently.

*Evolution in your playing is crucial to your performance.*

Yeah, it definitely is. My playing changes all the time from tour to tour. I see things in a different light. For me, it's still very much a learning experience. A 16-year-old kid wrote me recently and said he was taking from a jazz/rock violin teacher who taught him how to play jazz and rock. I was like "Wow, I never heard of such a thing when I was coming up." That's cool; it's good because I think it will increase their interest in music and the violin in general. It may also make them more interested in classical music as well.

*To express themselves.*

Exactly. Piano players for years have been able to play Chopin, but they have also been able to play just like Fats Domino. They have that option of different styles of playing. But now with the violin, a lot more kids are getting interested because they're saying, "Hey, I can do something that rocks a little bit, that is a little bit more fun."

*When are you at your best?*

I'm at my best when I'm on tour, on the road. When we get to the stage that night, I'm home. In a lot of ways I feel more comfortable there than I do anywhere else. I work out probably three hours a day. That is also a big part of getting me in the right place to be at my best. It clears my head; it helps to get my creative juices going for the journey ahead.

*Any advice to up-and-comers?*

Practice and listen to your teacher. The most important thing I would say is just to have fun and realize that music is about having fun and about expressing what's in your heart and soul, and it's about feeling. Have fun and enjoy what you do. Keep jamming.

# Equipment Roundup

On the road, we've got four Zeta Boyd Tinsley Models—two violins are tuned to a standard tuning: a main one and a backup. For the song "Stay," we tune the E string to F—again, one is the main and the other the backup. To make the Boyd Tinsley model, Zeta took a violin he liked the sound of and measured the actual bridge. On the bridge, each finger that reaches up to a string has a pickup in it. They measured the apoxy around the pickup because we believe that affects sound. So, the bridge on the Boyd Tinsley model is the same as his favorite sound.

There is a Zeta Strados Violin with Custom Tuners sometimes used as a backup. This is what Boyd calls the Fiddolin because it has the mandolin tuners. This was a violin he used before the Boyd Tinsley Model was built.

A Furman PL-8 Power Conditioner supplies raw wattage and power. We've got a Korg DTR-1 Digital Tuner, an API 500HPR pre-amp, and a Coleman Audio Switcher.

We carry around six Shure U4D-UB wireless units. What's unique about these is that the transmitter is built into the violin. He doesn't need a belt pack.

He uses a lot of settings on his Eventide GTR-4000 Ultra Harmonizer, but they are mainly reverbs and some pitch shift.

There are Trace Acoustic TA200s on stage, but he technically goes direct. The main reason they are on stage is that the bass rig is so huge that it would be empty on his side. On stage he's got the Sensaphonics ear monitors from Michael Santucci out of Chicago.

We change strings everyday. It's crazy, but if I don't, he'll break them. He uses Thomastick Dominant strings, *mittel* gauge.

*Erik Porter*

# The Best of What's Around

**from** *Under the Table and Dreaming*

**Words and Music by**
**David J. Matthews**

Copyright © 1994 Colden Grey, Ltd. (ASCAP)
International Copyright Secured   All Rights Reserved

### Post-chorus Riff

In this Post-chorus Riff, the violin plays the same rhythm as the rest of the band—try to "feel" this groove. The chorus itself has a "spacy" synth feel to it; try to emulate the sound with echo and reverb. Notice that this tune is in the key of A and uses the Mixolydian scale with an added flat 6.

**0:39**

### Post-chorus Riff/Outro Riff Combo

This riff immediately follows the Post-chorus Riff at the end and doubles the vocal melody. The goal is to imitate the vocal phrasing, but take a moment to check out the sax solo. Try playing along to match and learn the phrasing.

**3:03**

# What Would You Say

**from** *Under the Table and Dreaming*

**Words and Music by**
**David J. Matthews**

Copyright © 1994 Colden Grey, Ltd. (ASCAP)
International Copyright Secured   All Rights Reserved

### String Line Riff

This A Mixolydian riff sings behind the John Popper harmonica solo. Play this one with nice, long, legato bows for smoothness.

**2:52**

The main guitar riff is also interesting chop fodder, plus good practice for your transcribing skills. It's based on an A9 chord using the Mixolydian scale with an added 9th—check it out and try to play it on the violin. You might also want to experiment with the sax and harmonica solos as good work-outs for your funk chops.

# Satellite

from *Under the Table and Dreaming*

**Words and Music by**
**David J. Matthews**

Copyright © 1994 Colden Grey, Ltd. (ASCAP)
International Copyright Secured   All Rights Reserved

### Intro Guitar Riff

It just can't hurt to learn this guitar riff—it's got a great classical feel that is well suited to strings. Try it both *pizzicato* and *arco*.

**0:00**

### Violin Intro Riff

This is the string ornamentation above that Intro Guitar Riff. Play it with a gentle, flowing bow arm.

**0:23**

### Scalar Riff

It's duet time with the soprano sax. Play this Mixolydian scale riff with the same smoothness as the intro riff. Notice how Dave Matthews interconnects each section of the song with string lines.

**2:41**

# Rhyme & Reason

from *Under the Table and Dreaming*

**Words and Music by**
**David J. Matthews**

Copyright © 1994 Colden Grey, Ltd. (ASCAP)
International Copyright Secured   All Rights Reserved

## Bridge Riff

Play this interval of a 5th brashly—think of it as a "violin power chord"! This type of double stop is useful when you need more sound, so really dig into the strings. It's as though this line is playing the part of a Motown R & B horn section.

**0:48**

## Duet Riff (with Sax)

Try mimicking the sax articulations and make sure to give the beginning of each note some real bite.

**1:12**

## "Spacey" Second Verse Riff

Play with lots of reverb and echo for that cool, "spacey" sound.

**1:44**

# Typical Situation

from *Under the Table and Dreaming*

**Words and Music by
David J. Matthews**

Copyright © 1994 Colden Grey, Ltd. (ASCAP)
International Copyright Secured   All Rights Reserved

### Main Guitar Riff

This is the main guitar riff of the song, but a *pizzicato* approach turns it into a fun string line. If you own a five-string violin, try playing it down the octave.

# Dancing Nancies

from *Under the Table and Dreaming*

**Words and Music by
David J. Matthews**

Copyright © 1994 Colden Grey, Ltd. (ASCAP)
International Copyright Secured   All Rights Reserved

### Intro Pizzicato Riff

Here's another riff that's well suited to *pizz.* strings. Boyd moves the violin from its classical perch at the chin and plays it by his waist, guitar-style.

### Double Stop Chorus Riff

These double stops involve a simple back-and-forth motion with the bow. Think of this as an imitation of a "rhythm accordion" part.

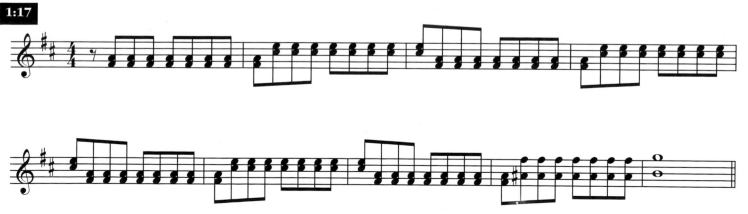

### Verse Riff

Boyd is an expert at picking out complementary counterpoint parts. Be sure to use lots of reverb and keep things legato.

**2:08**

# Ants Marching

from *Under the Table and Dreaming*

Words and Music by
**David J. Matthews**

Copyright © 1994 Colden Grey, Ltd. (ASCAP)
International Copyright Secured   All Rights Reserved

### Intro Riff

Here's the tune's main riff pattern—a little motif that doubles with the soprano sax. Don't forget to bend your second finger and emphasize that "fiddley" sound.

**0:03**

### Trade-Off Duet

Here are the "trade-offs" with the sax player—one measure per instrument. Boyd keeps within the D major pentatonic scale (D, E, F#, A, B)—don't forget to really scrub your bow on the string to get that country feel.

**0:55**

## Chorus Riff

It's just a little D major scalar riff, but this "mini flourish" acts as a great segue in several parts of the tune.

**1:12**

## Fiddle Breakdown Solo

Here's a great example of a traditional breakdown fiddle solo, and Boyd's strengths really show themselves in these sections. Notice that the band is just hitting the downbeats of the chords in each measure. After you've mastered this solo, try riffing on your own using the D major pentatonic scale—don't forget to include lots of slides and double stops.

**3:22**

# Lover Lay Down

from *Under the Table and Dreaming*

**Words and Music by
David J. Matthews**

Copyright © 1994 Colden Grey, Ltd. (ASCAP)
International Copyright Secured   All Rights Reserved

## Intro Riff

This beautiful melody is played by the soprano sax, yet it is equally well suited to the violin.

**0:05**

# Jimi Thing

## from *Under the Table and Dreaming*

**Words and Music by**
**David J. Matthews**

Copyright © 1994 Colden Grey, Ltd. (ASCAP)

### Violin Solo

Rock on! Here's a solo based on the G major pentatonic scale (G, A, B, D, E). Use plenty of distortion here—milk that guitar sound and phrasing for as much as you can. The slides that Boyd uses are particularly important for the rock guitar feel, so make sure they're rock solid and in tune.

**3:19**

# Warehouse

## from *Under the Table and Dreaming*

**Words and Music by**
**David J. Matthews**

Copyright © 1994 Colden Grey, Ltd. (ASCAP)

### Fiddle-style Riff

The violin here adds to the overall tone color of the section. A little distortion and reverb can go a long way, so be careful that the individual notes don't get lost in the blur. Let the A string ring out as much as possible, especially when this riff is repeated during the fade out at the end of the tune.

**1:23**

## Pizzicato Calypso Riff

This riff fits right in with the calypso feel that begins about halfway through the tune. Let go and have fun!

**4:14**

# #34

from *Under the Table and Dreaming*

Music by David J. Matthews,
Leroi Moore, Carter Beauford
and Haines Fullerton

## Guitar Riff

You can emulate the guitar or the sax here by playing *pizzicato* or *arco*, respectively.  Try going through the passage through each way, and then fly with whichever feels best to you.

**0:00**

# So Much to Say

from *Crash*

Words and Music by
David J. Matthews, Boyd Tinsley
and Peter Griesar

## Chorus Riff with Baritone Sax

That's the baritone saxophone playing along. Bow the notes short and fast—think of the brass work in any number of Motown tunes. This baritone sax and violin combo sound is rather unique to the Dave Matthews Band.

**1:07**

### Bridge Riff with Baritone Sax

Here's an effective counterpoint to the baritone sax part. Use a clean tone, play as smoothly as possible, and be aware that most of the A-string notes match up rhythmically with snare hits.

# Two Step

**from *Crash***

**Words and Music by
David J. Matthews**

Copyright © 1993, 1996 Colden Grey, Ltd. (ASCAP)
International Copyright Secured   All Rights Reserved

### Pizzicato Solo Riff

This little *pizzicato* melody adds a skewed country feel to this otherwise moody tune. You can play along with the offbeats to participate in the groove.

### Pizzicato Bridge Riff

Here's another *pizz.* riff. The vocal weaves in and out of this D minor solo that centers around the 1st and 5th degrees scale.

## Sunny Pizzicato Riff

This A Phrygian scale riff has a sunny, major mode feel that contrasts with the earlier atmosphere.

## Octave Pizzicato Riff

This riff takes us right back into that D minor, moody tone from earlier in the tune. It may be easier to play the violin away from your chin, guitar-style—finger with your left hand and pluck with your right.

# Too Much

from *Crash*

**Words by David J. Matthews**
**Music by David J. Matthews, Carter Beauford,**
**Stefan Lessard, Leroi Moore and Boyd Tinsley**

### Intro/Transition Riff

Get down and funky! This riff is also used as a transition elsewhere in the tune.

# Too Much cont.

## Duet with Baritone Sax

Real swamp water! Inject this duet with lots of big band flavor and match the articulation of the baritone sax by using short and punchy bow strokes.

**1:32**

## Fiddle-style Solo

This solo riff also appears later—check out all the improvisation at the end of the tune. Feel free to experiment—just let the open E string ring out as much as you can. And scrub that violin!

**2:05**

# #41

**from *Crash***

**Words by David J. Matthews**
**Music by David J. Matthews, Carter Beauford,**
**Stefan Lessard, Leroi Moore and Boyd Tinsley**

Copyright © 1996 Colden Grey, Ltd., Carter Beauford, Stefan Lessard,
Leroi Moore and Boyd Tinsley (ASCAP)
International Copyright Secured   All Rights Reserved

## Sax Duet Riff

This jazzy little riff doubles the sax line. Don't be afraid to let it swing, and remember to slide up to the first note.

**1:11**

*Play 8 times*

## Violin Solo

This extended solo works great over the cool reggae groove.

**3:33**

# Say Goodbye

from *Crash*

Words and Music by
David J. Matthews

### Chorus Riff

This Chorus Riff, which provides a poignant counterpoint to the vocals, should be played very lyrically and sweetly—but be careful not to overdo the effect.

**3:09**

# Drive In Drive Out

from *Crash*

Words and Music by
David J. Matthews

### "Urgent" Violin Verse 1 Riff

Feel that 6/8 groove, match the bold and urgent feel coming from the rest of the band, keep a steady bow arm, and play the notes as evenly as possible.

**0:46**

### Chorus Riff

Keep those rhythms nice and clean while you rock out on this intense little riff.

**1:56**

*Play 3 times*

## Interlude Riff

This funky riff makes for a great syncopated groove and an interesting segue into the Verse that follows. Don't lose the beat!

**3:35**

# Let You Down

from *Crash*

**Words by David J. Matthews**
**Music by David J. Matthews and Stefan Lessard**

Copyright © 1996 Colden Grey, Ltd. and Stefan Lessard (ASCAP)
International Copyright Secured   All Rights Reserved

## Chorus Riff

This smooth triplet feel doubles the guitar—play it in 3rd and 1st positions and be generous in your slurring in order to create a true legato feel.

**1:32**

# Lie in Our Graves

from *Crash*

Words by David J. Matthews
Music by David J. Matthews, Carter Beauford,
Stefan Lessard, Leroi Moore and Boyd Tinsley

## Unison Duet with Guitar

Play those triplet figures cleanly—don't just throw them away—and make sure you're in absolute rhythmic sync with the guitar part.

**1:09**

## Violin Solo Riff

The solo is played over a D chord feel. Experiment using D Mixolydian (D, E, F♯, G, A, B, C) and A Dorian (A, B, C, D, E, F♯, G).

**1:26**

# Tripping Billies

from *Crash*

**Words and Music by**
**David J. Matthews**

## Intro Riff

Here's a nice, strong riff played with the band. Make sure you key into the unison feel and watch out for those anticipations. Don't come in too late!

**0:06**

# Pantala Naga Pampa

from *Before These Crowded Streets*

**Words and Music by**
**David J. Matthews**

## Violin Riff

This sweet melody floating on top of the rest of the ensemble is very effective. Make sure to keep everything legato.

**0:17**

# Rapunzel

from *Before These Crowded Streets*

**Words and Music by
David J. Matthews, Stefan Lessard
and Carter Beauford**

Copyright © 1997 Colden Grey, Ltd. (ASCAP)
International Copyright Secured   All Rights Reserved

## Intro Riff

The 5/4 time signature is very effective in setting up the tone of the song. Make sure you know where beat 1 is at all times, don't let the time signature change throw you, and be sure to really saw with the bow on those 16th notes.

**0:00**

*Play 7 times*

# The Last Stop

from *Before These Crowded Streets*

**Words and Music by
David J. Matthews and Stefan Lessard**

Copyright © 1997 Colden Grey, Ltd. (ASCAP)
International Copyright Secured   All Rights Reserved

Pick up the five-string for this one. This little tune has a very interesting Middle Eastern flavor and contains some great violin gems throughout. The scale used is actually the Hebrew Ahovah-Rabboh scale (F♯, G, A♯, B, C♯, D, E). Check out some great Indian violinists like L. Shankar and L. Subramian for further listening and information on this great scale.

## Intro Riff

The trill adds an important flourish to the riff. In most Middle Eastern styles of playing, the ornaments, trills, and turns add necessary color. This riff returns both in this form and others throughout the song.

**0:00**

## Verse Riff

Here's a little variation on the Intro Riff used in the verses.

**0:08**

# Don't Drink the Water

Here's another great vibe—a Cajun-injected funk tune that features Bela Fleck's great banjo playing. Try doubling him with *pizzicatos* on your violin. In the second Verse, there's a very cool rhythm violin part using wah-wah and distortion—check it out.

## Verse Riff

This totally relaxed scrub adds to the general ambiance.  Don't be timid here—saw away with the bow.

**0:17**

## End Riff

This is the dark riff that plays in the background of the vocals. Follow Dave's lead and give this line a real rhythmic bite.

**5:03**

# Stay (Wasting Time)

## "Makes You Wanna" Riff

Try and master this violin version of that funky sax line. Use *spiccatto* bowing—play off the string and real short.

**2:19**

## Interlude Riff

Here's another great funk line played along with the band.

**2:22**

23

# Halloween

**from *Before These Crowded Streets***

**Words and Music by**
**David J. Matthews**

Copyright © 1993 Colden Grey, Ltd. (ASCAP)
International Copyright Secured   All Rights Reserved

This is perhaps the most innovative track the Dave Matthews Band has every attempted. The addition of the Kronos Quartet is brilliant—the added strings really create a very original tune. Listen closely to the great string arrangement done by John D'Earth and you'll hear some really cutting-edge string ideas.

## Intro Riff

Shades of *The King and I* meet something much, much creepier. Slide into that spooky vibrato.

## Verse Riff

That Intro Riff reappears in various permutations, both whole and in part—here's one.

# The Stone

**from *Before These Crowded Streets***

**Words and Music by**
**David J. Matthews**

Copyright © 1997 Colden Grey, Ltd. (ASCAP)
International Copyright Secured   All Rights Reserved

Here's yet another tune featuring the Kronos Quartet.

## Unison Intro Riff

The strings double the guitar and repeat this little D minor riff into the verse. Don't be swayed by the "classical" sound of the quartet—go ahead and fiddle away.

### Outro Riff

We've slid into the relative major (F) by the time the Outro rolls around. Keep things very legato, very sweet, and very musical in this little riff that repeats several times through several different instrumental lines.

**5:47**

# Crush

**from *Before These Crowded Streets***

**Words and Music by David J. Matthews**

Dave employed the Kronos Quartet once again—this time, in a tune with a shufflin' beat.

### Chorus Riff

Maintain a "pushed" feel throughout this Chorus Riff, but don't neglect to be sprightly with those 16th notes.

**2:13**

Shuffle feel

# The Dreaming Tree

**from *Before These Crowded Streets***

**Words and Music by David J. Matthews and Stefan Lessard**

### Guitar Intro Riff

Try this repeating 7/8 guitar riff both *arco* and *pizz.* Either way, make it flow.

**0:00**

# Pig

from *Before These Crowded Streets*

**Words and Music by
David J. Matthews, Stefan Lessard,
Carter Beauford, Leroi Moore and Boyd Tinsley**

## Opening Riff

The violin leads this laid back opening quite nicely. When you're confident with this line, try some of your own improvisations over it in A major.

**0:01**

## Unison "Love" Riff

The whole band sticks to this rhythm here. Do I hear shades of "Eleanor Rigby"?

**3:06**

# Spoon

from *Before These Crowded Streets*

**Words and Music by
David J. Matthews**

## Melody Riff 1

This tune features some lovely, lyrical string work. Use a very clean sound to feature this clear melody with a loose, lazy feel.

**0:38**

# I Did It

from *Everyday*

**Words and Music by
David J. Matthews and Glen Ballard**

## Seque Riff

Keep the rhythms neat and clean in this D major riff. Watch those 5ths.

**1:55**

# When the World Ends

from *Everyday*

**Words and Music by**
**David J. Matthews and Glen Ballard**

Copyright © 2000 Colden Grey, Ltd. (ASCAP), Universal - MCA Music Publishing,
A Division of Universal Studios, Inc. and Aerostation Corporation (ASCAP)
International Copyright Secured   All Rights Reserved

### Intro Octave Riff

This riff compliments the main guitar groove at the top of the song and repeats several times under the vocal.

**0:00**

# The Space Between

from *Everyday*

**Words and Music by**
**David J. Matthews and Glen Ballard**

Copyright © 2000 Colden Grey, Ltd. (ASCAP), Universal - MCA Music Publishing,
A Division of Universal Studios, Inc. and Aerostation Corporation (ASCAP)
International Copyright Secured   All Rights Reserved

### Chorus Riff

The violin here doubles and, therefore, supports the guitar part. Keep this in mind and don't forget to slur the three-note motif in each repetition.

**0:23**

# Dreams of Our Fathers

**from *Everyday***

**Words and Music by**
**David J. Matthews and Glen Ballard**

Copyright © 2000 Colden Grey, Ltd. (ASCAP), Universal - MCA Music Publishing,
A Division of Universal Studios, Inc. and Aerostation Corporation (ASCAP)
International Copyright Secured   All Rights Reserved

### "Rhythmic Afterthought" Riff

This little "rhythmic afterthought" works well with the rhythm guitar. Keep the articulations nice and short—you may even wish to play it *pizz.* instead of *arco.*

**0:07**

# So Right

**from *Everyday***

**Words and Music by**
**David J. Matthews and Glen Ballard**

Copyright © 2000 Colden Grey, Ltd. (ASCAP), Universal - MCA Music Publishing,
A Division of Universal Studios, Inc. and Aerostation Corporation (ASCAP)
International Copyright Secured   All Rights Reserved

### Intro Sax-doubling Riff

Make sure you match the articulations of the baritone sax as closely as possible.

**0:00**

### Verse Riff

Keep the bowings long and legato. This background makes for a very effective contrast to the vocal.

**0:26**

### Chorus Riff

Here's a little happy-go-lucky riff that caps the ends of each chorus line. Slide and dip your left hand to create a loose feel.

**0:43**

29

# If I Had It All

from *Everyday*

Words and Music by
David J. Matthews and Glen Ballard

## Verse Riff

The violin doubles the piano here in this low riff. Play the double stops as in tune as possible and don't forget to include the finger slide.

0:06

# What You Are

from *Everyday*

Words and Music by
David J. Matthews and Glen Ballard

## Intro Riff

This riff with a slight Middle Eastern flair works well on the violin. Trills and other flourishes really add to the spicy flavoring of this tune—feel free to experiment!

0:17

*Play 4 times*

## Chorus Riff

The violin here fills out the chorus rhythm part. Play this short and evenly; it also makes a great exercise.

1:15

# Fool to Think

from *Everyday*

**Words and Music by**
**David J. Matthews and Glen Ballard**

### Intro Rifff

The music below incorporates both the sax and violin lines. You'll want to emulate both instruments and play this passage as smoothly as possible. Both recur elsewhere in the song.

`0:02`

### Chorus Riff

A time signature change propels us into this three-beat pattern that repeats over several measures. Don't lose track of beat 1!

`0:41`

# Sleep to Dream Her

from *Everyday*

**Words and Music by**
**David J. Matthews and Glen Ballard**

### Verse Riff

This violin line is a wonderful counterpoint to the percolating guitar rhythm. This is a 6/8 feel, so make sure that it swings, but don't lose the legato.

`0:20`

## Sleep to Dream Her cont.

### Interlude Riff

This goes along with the tenor sax part—a very "Pink Floyd-ian" vibe.

**1:22**

# Mother Father

**from** *Everyday*

**Words and Music by**
**David J. Matthews and Glen Ballard**

### Bridge Riff

This Latin-flavored tune includes this riff as a secondary pattern that repeats several times over the 12/8 feel. The tune is also a great song to jam over. Follow guest guitarist Carlos Santana's sense of development here—it's truly inspiring.

**1:53**

# Everyday

**from** *Everyday*

**Words and Music by**
**David J. Matthews and Glen Ballard**

### Chorus Riff

The violin is played through a wah-wah pedal to produce the funky tone. This riff pushes off the section change nicely; don't forget to step onto your pedal and really rock out.

**0:56**